ROSALIND JANA

BRANCH + VEIN

Rosalind
Jana

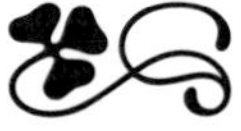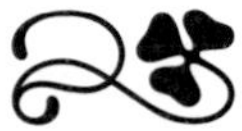

uncorrected proof

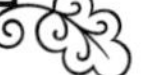

Uncorrected Proof
Copyright © Rosalind Jana
First published in 2016
by New River Press London

thenewriverpress.com

set in Mrs Eaves
design and typesetting
by New River Press
cover photo Andrew Fusek Peters

ISBN: 978-0-9954807-1-1

For my parents— for their excellent family stories, and
their willingness to tell when my poems need more work.

ICE

First step treads from the ebb of hills.
A careful step, chosen to balance up
this back of mine, new-lined by metal.

Geese are flecked arrows loosed
from the lake's glass table.
"The biggest freeze in years,"
according to Stu — and he'd know.
He's lived here all his life.

A line of purple snagged satin
runs down my spine.
Neck to waist,
a numb seam, stitched,
flesh zipped tight.
Walking is still a sea-sickness,
rising through choppy waves.

I wade, determined, each morning, with my dad,
to the lake where paths
are held by thin scribbled bushes.
We pace a little further
every day.

First step treads from the ebb of hills.
Second step starts with a tap on the ice.
Boot held, pressure-less.
Weight is trusting.
We throw stones and they skitter,
denting the sweep ahead.
Three strides out are a faith.
My heavy shoulders quiver.
The blades are sails.

To stand while rooks echo,
see branches furred in frost;
to keep feet still on solid nothing,
look back to the shore of brittle reeds,
is to be reversed,
like breathing backwards.

TRANSPARENT

She stands with arms held up,
face fixed, feet forward,
heart and lungs on show:
transparent woman
cased in plastic skin,
with a placard by her toes.

Red and blue vein themselves
over intestines that do not function.
They are for show, illustrating
intimacies common to us all.

Imagine if we, who
scrutinized this still body,
wandering around
the Wellcome Collection,
were stripped back too —
clothes dissolved and flesh
like glass, insides visible
to others' eyes:
the thud of valves and squeeze of blood,
each filling of lungs to give us speech -
witnessed as they did their work,
like nothing more unusual
than the blink of an eye
or smacking of wet lips.

But where this form
has bright insides, ours would be
as meat — brown and bloody,
not pink, green, orange.
A uniform to function well,
each bone connected, muscle
linked, organs on their constant shift.

All hums in hiding day by day,
We move. That hollowed shape will stay.

BALANCE

There, where there might be a queue or empty space —
a girl, upside down, poised between
two tables, wrists held taut
one hand each side of the bench's back,
feet flipped up toward the beams.

We pause, watching this unexpected
spectacle balanced among
mugs and laptops — clatter of café
stilling to a hush as
she raises, lowers, tilts to the left,
lifts one hand, flourishing
her command of gravity.

How can she occupy the air
with such fluency —
assuming levity like it was as natural
as standing up?
We envy her, caught
for a second in
heels over head suspension,
and applaud
the return to ground.

HOLLOW

He was a dent in the sofa,
hollowed to fit in the corner;
at the other end, two dips: heels left in felt.

We could not fill these cavities.
Only his stoop might —
elbows sagging into cushions each morning.
We sat in other places,
avoided the shadows cast
by our father.
He left himself behind, dwindled
to blank eyes, trembling hands.

Fearing the January cold
he bound the living room round with heat
thick as boiled wool, tight at the neck.

"I'm sorry", he said, "so sorry."
Our chatter tried to fill his gaps.
We edged through days, orbited the empty space
of absence.

Our mother stacked his walking boots
under stairs.
His overcoat hung in the dark,
velvet collar waiting for a warm body
to fill it up.

He tried to fold himself away,
But could not curl small enough
to pass unseen.

Dust settled as days passed; months marked by
deeper hollows until, with such slowness

of bare twigs edging into leaf,
cool air spooled the house.

Upholstery dents receded.
We pulled on coats, slipped feet in boots,
and took small steps
imprinting softly into hills.

JUMP

The grass has an over-ripe thickness,
Damping ankles that dare
toward the lake;
an under-hum of fly and midge.

Near the gate something snags,
drags glance down to
a scatter of brown-flecked
flicks - movement registered
before the frogs themselves.

Hundreds. Thumbnail-tiny.
The usually smooth road alive —
full with shifts and jerks,
dull sparks on tarmac
as muscles flex and legs stretch for
leaps the length of a paperclip.

I tread with care,
afraid my clumping boots will
flatten handfuls.
Their scale scares.
Each step is potential murder.

Stride pared to an intricate tip-toe,
I weave — hopping with
none of their purpose or grace,
wobbily pirouetting past the lake,
each step calculated not to
squash the passage of
these annual commuters:
seething bodies
rushing about their
inches of business.

MOMENT

For a while, the moment has enough room
to feed itself, moment to moment.
We chose this for the beginning-middle-end
of each new afternoon or evening.
Sometimes a morning too. Then one of us,
after searching for underwear and shoes,
is kissed at the door: shutting the moment
behind them, carrying the smell of
the other while they walk home.

SCAR

The mark between my shoulder blades
is flesh zipped tight and thin,
a silver stripe of lavender that
stretches neck to waist.
See the thumb print dented
where the scalpel sliced my skin:
my back un-picked, then darned by threads
that seamed and stitched and laced.
Between the cut and sewing up
my mind was shuttered murk,
anaesthetized to lie inert
as bone and nerve were bared,
muscle stripped by surgeon's hands,
my meaty spine his work,
the twisted cord of vertebrae
a darkness to be dared.

Undressed of skin for five stiff hours
this blood-webbed gap was lined
with metal rods, with hooks, with screws,
to force my backbone straight.
A two inch gain as curves were stretched —
a permanent unwind
of willful bone once bent skewwhiff,
now pinned with heavy weight.
From carpentry to seamstressing
as skin became a cloak
to cover up the scaffolding
that left my body raw.
A needle sewed a score of red.
At six o'clock I woke,
The morphine black blown out by light,
my back already sore.

A satin streak now marks the months
suspended in my pain.
Recovery has been condensed
to tissue pearled and taut.
The spine beneath solidified,
this overlay a stain
of contoured flesh now fading quick,
a puckered afterthought.

GHOST

We were talking of folklore.
I paused, named the first to come
to mind: 'The White Lady of Walcott.'
She smiled. "Don't you recall?
That one's mine"

Oh, the gossip's there alright:
the smooth sweep of a
see-through woman from
country house to village church,
drifting her way over the lake
like so much early morning mist.
A translucent heirloom:
comes with the territory.

But my mother's version,
created for stage, is tailored
with made-up detail:
outlines a drowning on a sunny day,
heavy skirts, weak branches,
a husband intent on
disposing of his pretty, young wife.

A life that almost certainly happened
somewhere. Not here though.
We know nothing about this whisper
of a figure, etching her
back-and-forth route through trees
and walls: as insubstantial
as the version dreamt up for a play
a few miles away in a dusty school hall.

TOMATOES

Warm earth tang of tomato vines
thickens the greenhouse, lending it
a sweetness. Diana has her basket.
She picks. No order to her choices.
I get the split ones. They are sun, earth,
a tongue-curling burst of life. Her hands,
skin like crumpled bedsheets,
are deft. One could not leave without this
ritual: the pluck and bite, world beyond glass
ebbing, here only green, yellow, orange, red.
I am sent off with a box of wind-fall
apples and a lettuce, soil still clinging
to its roots.

AWAKE

Night-noise trickles in:
voices, cars, plumbing, laughter.
Drops of sound in the hot dark.
Slow breaths behind my shoulders,
one settled arm scooped around my waist,
palm pressed to stomach.
We shift — rolling apart,
spine to spine, foreheads pressed,
legs a slot of knees and shins.
A slow tug of war as the duvet twists,
my fidget-dance of flips and shifts
calculated - his slow rolls instinct.

He rests with ease. I stay aware,
stuck with breeze and breaths and thoughts
too lucid for this outlined room,
begrudging his obliviousness.
Now and then I dip, eyes droop,
gaps and blanks, odd scenes, half-dreams
slipping in amongst my watch of windows,
bookshelves, the boxes stacked above
the wardrobe.

I can't explain this wakefulness.
Just restless heat, perhaps,
or the whirring murmur
of a mind too full to fall asleep,
time unhitched
from clocks and phones,
no way of knowing how
many hours to go.

ROOTS

This task requires keen eyes, plastic gloves,
and a toothbrush. Not new, mind. The kind
no longer needed — bristles worn thin enough
to justify their coat of red.

You bend your head,
offering up a scalp for my perusal,
inviting some small sense of revelation
in this act of witness, of searching out
your age: streaks of
grey, silver, salt-and-pepper
unearthed from hiding.

It's an affirmation, really.
You're defined so clearly by this shade
maintained for more than thirty years.
The thought of anything other than
"my mum with the red curls"
is impossible.

I cover each patch methodically,
scrutinizing your roots,
rubbing in colour
like someone touching up a painting,
sprucing fade into full glory,
and moving on,
completing this slap-dash ritual,
returning you to the version we know best.

HILLSIDE

There used to be roofs —
enough to keep six thousand heads
safe, warm, dry. Each house
the same: solid, square,
animals below, family upstairs.
Among them - chapels, a school,
churches too: concave buildings bearing up
the float of prayer,
where Orthodox belief once ruled.

Paint still clings in chalky traces,
soft blues, clay reds:
lingering stain of sky and earth.
The stones hold little now but thyme,
sage, poppies, thorns,
insects and quiet grief —
or is it peace? This stillness
is hard to read, wildflowers
a fresh crust on old rifts.

Nearly a century of empty rooms
opened up to light and rain:
an "exchange" the only nod to cracks,
one line snuck in by rules and entry fees
on the tourist board by the road.
The word suggests a switch, a swap,
reciprocal shift from Greek to Turk —
no mention made of treaties, wars,
a fifty minute slot of grace,
no more to spare, for everyone to
grab and gather, pack up, go, leave
the view they woke to each day,
the paths they scrambled down
to work the fields, that church

that cradled worship tight.

In under an hour, loss stooped in
and scooped them up,
one finger pointing over the mountain to
the nearest port — thin road peopled briefly
with bags, clothes, children, lives squeezed
down to possessions heaved on shoulders.

Other stories still are told, whispers
of conscription, their boys
snatched up and marched away as soldiers.
But let us leave what is unearthed,
stuck beneath the tongues of those who saw and knew.

Today we stand, caught
within the grass and walls — each
corner yielding up more homes
bedded into slopes that curve and
reach for clouds. There is a calm,
a soundlessness,
the window frames and chimney hollows
give us nothing. Only rocks,
full of words, tales, laughter, screams and song,
mosaic of sounds assembled — gone.
"Ghost town" it's called, but ghosts are too loud
for this hot, stony hill.
Absence has settled.

STARLINGS

They wheel and duck through swathes of grey
like iron filings — drawn to a point,
exploding outward, scattering sky.
Not quite a flock. More a congregation
singing quietly over the hills, winged specks
of grit lifted above anything we can reach.

They hang, hover, dart, spiral, spilling themselves
into each new moment. Patterns dissolve.
Brief correlations of wing and feather shift.
Stuck below, staring up, we're struck
by sheer theatre, played out for no-one in particular.

They climb, dip, climb again, rising in formation,
reaching heights that, from the ground, look boundless.
We stand, quiet, lifted with them,
witnessing this small glory,
caught in swoops and falls, soaring
for a second on flecks of flight,
cradled in the glooming light.

ROUTES

Roads and footpaths mark the land
like thread, securing each hill to the next.
Mapped, they're more like veins flushed with ink.
A neat anatomical sketch of breadth and shape,
the county's windy, bustling sweep of
fields, trees, traffic jams, town centers full with
late-night shouts, birds wheeling in flight,
trout splashing upriver, factories wheezing,
families arguing, the clatter of primary schools
at lunch, soft silence of empty houses,
lone walkers, dogs yapping, siblings laughing,
phones going, pheasant shooting ringing through valleys,
the early morning click of a camera capturing a deer,
reduced to a few, thin lines, names, sites of interest.
Paper proportions are so quiet,
so easily contained, the world expanding as far
as those four edges take it. Place thumb and finger on A
and B.
Imagine the life that stretch could hold, unfolded bit by
bit.
Trace it.

QUEUE

Behind you they stand, mum and grandma —
with you it's a three-strong queue
of single children, each no sibling
there to share the weight
their parents placed on shoulders
much too young.

Three twirl-haired women, thin lips set strong,
with steel backbones holding straight
a tailored load.

For one, the vicar's daughter, the dull
understanding that others came first,
that she was the girl on show,
an actor put before the parish.
The slow monotony of being good,
resentment like a scratch not seen
but itched in private,
blotching red while paper smiles
hid the ache
of quiet denial.
Married to a boy who first held her
as a newborn, while their parents
mapped out future years,
plotting her world before
she could speak.

Next up, the rebel, stifled
by narrow eyes and curt remarks,
mother's tongue and father's kind constraint.
Her first engagement forced to break —
a Catholic incompatible
with their ideals. The split from home
was marked. Another man,

too shy, too neat,
was grabbed, the match
quite wrong but quick enough
to whisk away this flighty girl.
She sought divorce
with a child of one.
They fought long.
She won.

Then you, on the move
From place to place,
Still ferried unwilling to daddy's dolls' house
for half of every holiday,
your say not heeded.

Love provided, yes,
but chaos too —
uncertainty the background hue
of each new wall,
the new-called 'home' often with another
stepdad in tow.
Your adolescence? More adult than fair
as your mum blew milkshake bubbles,
went barefoot, dared to remain young as
you grew up.

Look at the queue again.
Accumulated life on life,
each docked into what went before.

But here plots change.

In front of you
stands not one, but two.
A pair.
Five years between
this boy and girl, with legs

stretched past your smaller height.
We are not lined, but side by side.
With years ahead and tales behind,
our weight no more than words
passed on — these stories
ours to tell in turn
without the bulk you had to hold,
that hoarded store of care and cold.

SWINGING

Past a certain point, you are not
meant to swing
- admire it, maybe —
nod at the sight of that plank
suspended in the early evening.
You are too old for such
sweet childishness.
Nearly grown up.

But there it is, hanging,
the sharp soil smell
of green around.
Tacked on the edge of this wood
like an afterthought —
but not,
for the chain is new,
strung where rope once frayed,
two strong lines slicing the view ahead.

There's no-one around.
None to see if you just
sit, sink down with hands
curled on the cold links,
elbows tucked in.

None to see if you lift your heels,
testing weightlessness,
the give of air.

None to see that darting kick,
quick, the swish as legs stretch up,
toes pushed above the flat and
higher -
leaftops just beyond

your small swoop reach.

Then slow, slower,
motion falling to a pause.
Ground returns,
right angled with heavy feet.

No-one saw. You can walk
away, leaving the swing
to a rattling still.

PATTERN

Patterns stick. This proximity
of knees was once a precursor
to closer things. We carry on
with familiarity, even as we tacitly
concede how our once-easy
intimacy has changed.

It's just that our bodies haven't quite
caught up. They need longer to adjust
to the distances we've agreed on.
Five months of knowing each
other's shoulders, hands, tongues,
doesn't dislodge itself on the day
of deciding that it's done.

IF

Six months on

I wake at 6.30am with a
'what if' strung between my teeth.
It curls around me, under the duvet,
a world of maybe and could-have-been
and if, if, if.

How can it be this perfect? To
know that our imagined other endings
are spun from shinier stuff than
we might have made, to know
that the knowing is enough:
that now we don't wake next to
each other, ever, we can both admit
we've lingered, separately,
on what our possibilities held,
and left them there.

BLUEBELLS

A blue hush surrounds us,
6pm light skimming limbs and leaves.
Nothing bad can happen here.
The still, warm wood is ours for playing.
Four sets of feet weave through the blue,
keen to not crush a stem, a head,
a faultless, tiny bell.
Here is our early-evening kingdom,
decked for welcome, hidden
just beyond the field's edge.
Perhaps we should never leave,
treading endlessly, climbing trees,
curling up in sprays of blue, knowing that here,
here all is well. We are caught in this
coppered slant of sun and branch.
But return we must. This kingdom is
not for living in. The calm is only ours
for this perfect hour's owning.

DRESS

Once upon a time
it was ivory satin, sitting
on a market stall,
waiting, presumably, for
another bride to fill its shape -
not expecting to be plucked up
with plans for reinvention,
taken home, dunked in the sink,
red dye seeping,
sluicing creamy shine to… pink.
Dreams of scarlet bias-cut
flames dimmed, the dress
- when rinsed —
blushing in a rose-cheeked blotch.

Ruined? No, but marred enough
to consign it to the dressing-up box.
No extra weddings for this now too-brash gown.
Its duties changed to smaller tasks,
outings arranged by the child of the house,
plucking up her mother's failed
attempt to add fire to snow.
It became a princess dress, a mermaid's
flesh, an honorable lady's attire:
the bow at the back holding each new
body that took it on.

Then, one day, the spell reversed,
colour weeping out
like juice from meat.
Water ran clear, eventually.
A magic trick, as if the pink
had never been there, like the
dress was as new as the day it had been
carried home.

HOTEL

It stands.
Hotel no more
on the sea-front.
Twenty-nine rooms in pink and yellow,
sagging curtains, sinks, coat hangers,
the soft unpeel of paint,
wallpaper curled like a fold in a page
left for reference.
The aging ceilings gape,
plaster dusting the carpet
in dandruff chunks,
liverspot stains mottled beneath.

All hidden behind a pale front door,
just one in a row of parallel, pebble-dashed
fronts, suspended in empty sleep.
It's a stone's-throw from arcades,
and seagulls, and waltzers sending
shrieks across the promenade.

In one room, a mirrored bar
throws back strange reflections,
selective glints of hand and lips —
nothing left, just blackcurrant squash;
crisp packets,
a glass untouched for twenty years.

In another, a sofa,
concave dip where someone once sat.
Nearby a hook like a beckoning finger,
dangles a single key
to a lock long lost.

The floors flourish up corridors,

the gauze of tatty net, an occasional
bed, shelf with odd contents
like malt vinegar, one sock, a clock,
fake flowers so ancient their plastic
heads have wilted, dropped.

It's a place where hollows grow.
Old sounds of feet and bells
and laughs and bickering hushed
from those before dissolved into
the quiet creaks and silent floors
where nothing stirs.

VEINS

As though someone painted her skin
while she slept — quick lines of ink,
invisible in normal light, left etched
on wrist and chest and feet:
illuminated under heat.

The shower's steam revealed her
roots, strings, rivers, webs,
wandering patterns washed with blue —
the odd violet accent.

Their surface nearness unnerved her,
skeins of arteries so close at hand.
She watched them in the mirror, held up
the inside dip of her elbow, scrutinized
each thigh, then checked her pulse:
dizzy with the quiet thud she alone
could lay claim to. It hummed
without effort, like breaths.

SCALE

The photo-album pages stick,
sounding like sellotape
when pulled apart.

First pregnancy, then scans, then me -
this tiny, scrunchy mass of
skin and little fists, hair-tufts,
tiny lips. A body small enough to fit
beneath a tea-towel, or cupped between
your two large hands — one at my head,
another curved to support my weight.

I curled on your chest:
a t-shirt cot that lulled me
with beats of breath and thumping heart —
that moment caught, stuck down,
still here for me to marvel at.

It's the scale I want to understand,
the way in which these legs that
let me reach top shelves and
bump against low ceilings could once
take up such scant space:
dimensions that now fill a bed
then minute —
your width, your height
allowing room to fold that scrap
of me so carefully under your coat,
unwrapping to show to neighbours the small
revelation of a living, sleeping baby.

Today I reach your shoulders,
head above others,
adjusted to this unfurled stature with its

wonky back, corkscrew hair,
long arms. Twenty years ago
I fitted the nook of your elbow, newly
introduced to this big world.

I move through it now,
sized up to navigate its scope,
with muscle enough to stride: early, little
me confined to slightly shiny rectangles,
snapshots stacked on pages,
hardly ever seen.

PATHS

Paths and roads can only guide
to half-there homes with unwrapped roofs,
messy floors of leaves and cans,
wooden struts like skeletons.

Paths and roads can only course
to rooms where trunks stretch through the shade,
doorways warped by storm and rain
hearths of broken planks and vines .

Paths and roads can only lead
to rusted nails and window frames
green-grown steps that lead to drops,
lichen-papered walls of rock.

I wander down these paths and roads,
taking pictures, noting views.
Treading through the settled ground
bending under broken gaps
and scaling branches reaching up.
Here I see those paths and roads,
rolling onwards, longwards, past,
and here I sit and write for those
who once lived here,
where these trees grow.

TABLE

Piled high like hopes,
packed tight in storerooms,
waiting for summer.

We are pushed into rows,
stand to attention for students
stretching our skinny metal legs
to relieve the cramp.
We warm ourselves
from cold months behind closed doors.

Answer booklets are placed on backs:
maths, science, history.
The questions change,
but the drumming fingers,
the jiggling knees and fidgety hands
never do.

Months of revision spilled onto pages
that scratch at our spines.
I envy their whisper-thin width,
want to ask if these sheets remember forests,
birds perched on branches, the slow drip
of thawing snow.
But the chance is felled
and they are swept away.

Each year I gain new tattoos.
"Tommy Davis is a dickhead."
"Fuck me, this sucks."
"That's what she said."
Biro hearts and squiggles:
no rings for me, but dates,
gossip, ink-scratched doodles

and the faint outline of a cock.

By June I'm worn out.
Am I "Clo loves Jack" or "Fozza 09"?
I dream of leaves, in this place where I'm weathered
by neither wind nor rain.

PMQ's

Obstacle course of noise,
jeers and whoops netting the room.
The only way to navigate this
weekly chorus is to shout louder —
cut through the rabble with
bellowing, sniggering, lung-splitting hollering.

Close your eyes. Listen
to its symphony.
Identify each sound in turn:
a laugh, a groan, a rising grumble,
sharp retorts, an insult poised and trembling.
Order called. Slick seconds of hush
for a question
(hear the titters)
an answer
(oh hear them erupt!)

A thunder of stamping,
benches shaking,
mudslide of cries,
calm down dear!
Don't worry though
no shrieks here.
That would be too
womanly a word.
This is pure testosterone yell,
voices shaped by bricks and coins
and good breeding.

Keep your eyes closed.
Think through the clatter.
Consider carefully.
Now, imagine the clothes.

Does all this racket belong
to suits, ties, polished shoes, green leather seats?
Or is it the echo of a classroom
on a hot summer's day:
frazzled teacher, boisterous rows
of bad haircuts and stuffy uniforms?

As my mother, the ex-teacher, once said:
"if an inspector saw that kind of behaviour,
the school would fail its Ofsted."

DEN

We arrived across the brook
with nettle-stung knees, bikes left on
the verge. Our hidden-nook home,
reworked with each new trip:
new dock-leaf rug, lumpy blanket graced
with veins. New cupboards hollowed out
of loose soil to hold our spoils from
the village shop. New sticks to mark our
boundaries, snapped from trees that formed
our roof. These living quarters made afresh:
grubs picked up, weeds stripped out.

We lived and played as runaways,
orphans ready to fend the world
with the aid of crisps, coke, penny sweets.
We stayed unseen — heads bobbing down
at each new rumble of an engine,
watching cars from behind brambles,
proud of our cunning.

Until, once, we tip-toed too far,
snapping daffodil heads to line our walls.
We stood in sight of an elderly neighbor,
her net-strung windows witness
to our impertinence.

She called it trespass.
We had to leave the ground and grass:
grew tall, grew up, left dens alone,
and now that corner is overgrown.

LECTURE

Head and shoulders rows of tweed
and fleeces, faded sweatshirts —
massed in khaki, navy, brown,
with one red jumper topped
by a grey cropped cut with a balding spot.

We're not a part of this set-up
with its stiff-back chairs and smell
of floorboards.
We're interlopers.
My heels and brimmed hat,
little brother in jeans,
hands cartooned with ink.
He won the history society essay prize.
Invited along to pick it up. Little did
we know how long this talk
would trudge.

Endless slides on steam power.
The man with a frown lodged in
by thick, square glasses
takes a breath, licks his fingers,
turns a lecture note and blinks again,
strained jokes delivered with expectation
of response — pauses flourished:
"As I'm sure you can see, it's in a
state of undress. The lagging was removed
due to asbestos!"

I didn't know such dullness could thrive,
nestled in creaking rows —
growing with each new remark.
"Now, here's my hero — a man who finally put
the water supply in London on a sensible footing."

We squirm, willing minutes to be malleable.
Finally we make our escape,
breathing in gaspfuls of the gorgeous
blue evening air. Wood-pigeons
fuss. The small town church bell
sings.

MEASURE

Biscuit musk filled your house,
rooms thick with heavy warmth,
When I stood at the same height
as you in your much-used armchair,
I reached at china figurines,
stroking Cinderella's lost shoes,
rubbing my thumb
on the bonnet of the shepherdess.

We passed glass boxes and vases as
you led me to the kitchen.
Here were treats — love measured out in
kitkats and coppers.

Kitkats plucked from the sideboard jar,
red paper ripped off for foil beneath.

Coppers heavy in their bag,
their load buckling small shoulders.

Tokens clutched in hot palms,
my fingers brushing your leaf-thin
skin.

Silver and bronze:
one fragile, one strong.

I refer to you as 'you':
Great-grandma
nearly nine-tenths of a century's strength.
Back when memory was solid
and you pulled me onto your lap to sing
"Sister Sarah eating chocolatera."

But as I stretched, you shrunk
Lowering yourself beneath my shoulders.
I bent down to listen, like Alice
out of step with these low stools and tables,
ungainly as I tip-toed past the lamps
and ornaments.

WOODS

Deep woods, tree roots, green moss,
onwards. A silver-grey film of drizzle.
'Rain' would be too solid a word
for this damp set of breaths that creeps
down necks and stiffens fingers.

Welsh woods, old routes, steep paths,
onwards. Walkers are flags dotting the
gloom with their anoraks, a brisk
one-two march as they scale banks
of leach-mulch, eyes ahead.

Wet woods, sharp smells, branch cracks,
onwards. We're dawdlers here, no
treks to undertake, our agenda sized down
to a flask, the odd laugh, some idle pursuit
of whatever lies beyond the corner.

Gold woods, bright twigs, clear air,
onwards. The slant of light appears
like a kiss — unexpected, picking
out detail, hollows illuminated,
the stream wrapping through the green.

Deep woods, welsh woods, wet woods,
gold woods, onwards.

MIRROR

We stand, doubled, at the pond's edge:
me and you. An inverted girl in blue by
your mirror twin: thick coat and green hat
perfectly matched. In the water, these quiet
replicas know nothing of our conversations:
the hour just stretched in comfort on a
sun-patched bench. They're oblivious to our
analysis, commiserations, unraveling of a
situation thread by thread. All they grab
are two young women, pausing to pull faces
and pose for each other's phones, chins tilted up.
We stand, doubled, at the pond's edge:
lingering for a minute, then disperse,
reverting just to us, no need to keep
these versions hanging from our ankles.

TAROT

The pack appears when the bottle
is half-drained. Brand new with
brilliance, it's William Blake, stained
glass and picture book illustration,
at once. The careful shuffle, mock
ritual of rectangles arranged on a
bedcover: fire and flowers, tides, faces.
Second time in a fortnight. Different
deck. Same assurances. We dip between
mirth and confession: each image
illuminated as we flick through the
pamphlet. It's not like me to take this
seriously: to willingly suspend the
rational. Yet its accuracy is strange,
promises so close to comfort.
Half, I know, just stuff that anyone could
fit: words a bowl to fill to brim
with something apt. But beyond that:
a kind of aligning, a recognition,
a wish for the order of a story so
easy to read, and believe.

TRAIN

(1) Red-gold glow on the First
Great Western train as it slides
into Reading. Burnt rose on blue.
Beyond: sinewed wires and rails
reaching into a sliver of sunset,
stretching like someone, sleep-eyed,
rising from a nap, cracking joints
and offering their fingertips to the sky.

(2) The pages are copper-orange,
cut through with a line of shadow
from the window's cross-hairs.
Black on bright. Outside,
a newly minted coin hangs
above the office blocks, offering
them a minute's wealth, before
the grey resumes.

(3) These seats do not smell of dust,
but they look like they should.
Some hold briefcases, newspapers,
laptops. Others wait for warm
thighs to cradle, slumped backs
to hold up. When I duck my head
to stare down the rows, I catch
ears, heels, elbows with sleeves
rolled up, and one phone:
held in a glowed echo of streetlamps.

(4) After the golden hour, the soft.
Black trees are trimmed with
pink marabou that blurs further up
again to blue. Above, a burning
half-sliver changes hands for silver,

and I am on the platform, people
pushing for home.

NEW RIVER PRESS

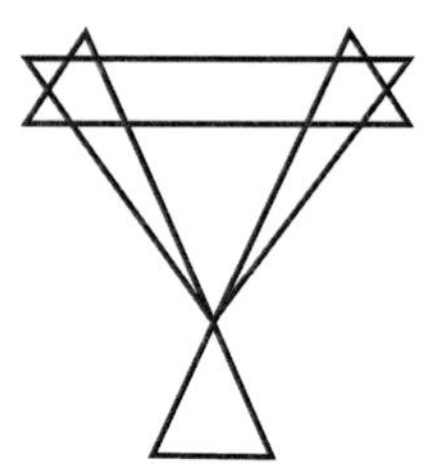

Fitzrovia
London